eggs

eggs

Great recipe ideas with a classic ingredient

>> in 60 ways

Marshall Cavendish
Cuisine

Design: Tan Shiang Chin
Photography: Jambu Studio

Copyright © 2006 Marshall Cavendish International (Asia) Private Limited

Published by Marshall Cavendish Cuisine
An imprint of Marshall Cavendish International
1 New Industrial Road, Singapore 536196

Limits of Liability/Disclaimer of Warranty: The Author and Publisher of
this book have used their best efforts in preparing this book. The Publisher
makes no representation or warranties with respect to the contents of this
book and is not responsible for the outcome of any recipe in this book.
While the Publisher has reviewed each recipe carefully, the reader may
not always achieve the results desired due to variations in ingredients,
cooking temperatures and individual cooking abilities. The Publisher
shall in no event be liable for any loss of profit or any other commercial
damage, including but not limited to special, incidental, consequential,
or other damages.

Other Marshall Cavendish Offices:
Marshall Cavendish Ltd. 119 Wardour Street, London W1F OUW, UK ·
Marshall Cavendish Corporation. 99 White Plains Road, Tarrytown NY
10591-9001, USA · Marshall Cavendish International (Thailand) Co Ltd.
253 Asoke, 12th Flr, Sukhumvit 21 Road, Klongtoey Nua, Wattana, Bangkok
10110, Thailand · Marshall Cavendish (Malaysia) Sdn Bhd, Times Subang,
Lot 46, Subang Hi-Tech Industrial Park, Batu Tiga, 40000 Shah Alam,
Selangor Darul Ehsan, Malaysia

Marshall Cavendish is a trademark of Times Publishing Limited

National Library Board Singapore Cataloguing in Publication Data

Eggs in 60 ways : great recipe ideas with a classic ingredient. – Singapore :
Marshall Cavendish Cuisine, c2006.
p. cm. – (In 60 ways)
ISBN-13 : 978-981-261-234-2
ISBN-10 : 981-261-234-3

1. Cookery (Eggs) I. Title: Eggs in sixty ways II. Series: In 60 ways

TX745
641.675 -- dc21   SLS2005053013

Printed in Singapore by Times Graphics Pte Ltd

contents >>

introduction >>

The most commonly used eggs in cooking are chicken eggs, although duck eggs may also be used. In comparison, duck eggs are larger and have yolks that are richer in colour and texture.

Eggs are high in protein, fat, calcium, iron and vitamins. They should be stored in a cool, well-ventilated place and eaten as fresh as possible. To test the freshness of an egg, place it, horizontally, in a bowl of cold water. If it stays horizontal, it is fresh. The more it rises to the vertical, the staler it is. Your sense of smell will also tell you if an egg is bad. For this reason, always break each egg into a small container before tipping it into the main mixing bowl or cooking pan.

Eggs may be prepared in so many ways that they need not become boring. They can be boiled (hard or soft), scrambled, fried, poached, baked or made into omelettes. Eggs are sometimes also eaten raw or cracked into a beverage and swallowed. Eggs are also a vital ingredient in many different recipes. Cakes, batter puddings and pancakes depend on the protein in eggs coagulating as they cook, and sauces, custards and tarts can be thickened by adding egg yolks. When vigorously whisked, egg whites hold large amounts of air and this increases their volume considerably. It is the air trapped in egg whites that give soufflés, sponges and mousses their light, airy texture, and that plays a vital role in the making of meringues.

Boiling Eggs

If using eggs that have been refrigerated, allow them to return to room temperature before use. To get soft-boiled eggs, place eggs in a pan of boiling water and leave for 1 minute, then turn off the heat, cover the pan and leave for 5 minutes. Alternatively, place eggs into a pan of boiling water and simmer for 3–4 minutes, depending on the size of the eggs.

For hard-boiled eggs, place eggs in a pan of hot water and return the water to the boil. Lower the heat and leave to simmer for 10 minutes. It is believed that stirring the eggs around in the water will cause the yolks to be centrally positioned, and thus be more aesthetically pleasing when sliced for serving. Remove the eggs from the pan and place into a basin of cold water to prevent the yolks from discolouring. Cooling the eggs this way will also make them easier to shell.

Varieties of Egg

Besides chicken and duck eggs, quail eggs are also commonly available. They are about a third the size of chicken eggs. On the other end of the scale are ostrich eggs, which are about 20 times bigger than chicken eggs. Although edible, they are not usually marketed.

Salted eggs are made from duck eggs. The fresh eggs are first coated with a paste made from clay, salt and water and then left for a few weeks. Salted eggs are usually sold still coated with the paste. Scrape it off and wash eggs well before using. If eaten whole, the salted eggs are hard-boiled. Salted egg yolks are also used as filling for Chinese pastries.

Century eggs are also made from duck eggs. Fresh duck eggs are covered in a paste of leaves, ash, lime, salt and water and then left to cure for a few weeks. Scrape off the paste and wash the eggs before using. The eggs can simply be shelled and eaten as an appetiser.

soups & appetisers

cheese soup with egg

This is a German dish, usually enjoyed with a loaf of crusty bread and a salad.

Serves 4

Ingredients

Egg yolks	4
Single (light) cream	160 ml (5 fl oz)
Cheddar cheese	55 g (2 oz), grated
Chopped fresh chives	2 Tbsp
Chicken stock	875 ml (29 fl oz / 3$\frac{1}{2}$ cups)

Method

- In a mixing bowl, beat egg yolks until they are well mixed. Beat in cream, cheese and chives.

- In a large saucepan, bring chicken stock to just under boiling point over moderate heat. Remove pan from heat and stir 90 ml (3 fl oz / 6 Tbsp) hot stock into egg and cheese mixture.

- Pour mixture into pan, stirring constantly. Return pan to low heat and cook, stirring constantly, until soup is thick and smooth. Do not let soup boil or it will curdle. Serve immediately with crusty bread.

egg balls in soup

These egg balls are an attractive addition to any clear soup. The egg balls may be prepared in advance, kept covered in the refrigerator, then cooked a few minutes before serving.

Serves 4

Ingredients

Hard-boiled eggs	4, shelled
Salt	$\frac{1}{4}$ tsp
Cayenne pepper	a dash
Chopped fresh parsley	1 tsp
Egg yolk	1, lightly beaten
Chicken stock	1 litre (32 fl oz / 4 cups)

Method

- Slice hard-boiled eggs in half and scoop out yolks. Rub yolks through a strainer into a bowl.
- Finely chop egg whites and add them to the bowl. Add salt, cayenne and parsley.
- With a fork, mash mixture and add enough raw egg yolk to make a stiff mixture.
- With your hands, shape mixture into small balls.
- Half-fill a medium-sized saucepan with water and bring to the boil over high heat. With a slotted spoon, place balls in boiling water and poach for 2 minutes.
- Meanwhile, bring chicken stock to the boil and ladle into 4 serving bowls.
- Remove poached balls from water using the slotted spoon and add a few to each bowl of soup. Serve immediately.

egg, noodle and cheese soup

This is one of the easiest and quickest of soups to prepare. Use canned chicken stock to reduce the hassle of preparing it from scratch.

Serves 4

Ingredients

Eggs	2
Salt	½ tsp
Ground black pepper	¼ tsp
Chilled chicken stock	1.25 litres (40 fl oz / 5 cups)
Egg noodles	55 g (2 oz), cooked
Grated Parmesan cheese	3 Tbsp
Chopped spring onions (scallions)	2 tsp

Method

- In a mixing bowl, beat eggs, salt, pepper and 125 ml (4 fl oz / ½ cup) chicken stock together with a wire whisk. Set aside.
- Pour remaining stock into a saucepan and add noodles and cheese.
- Place pan over high heat and bring stock to the boil. Reduce heat to low and whisk in egg mixture.
- Cook soup for 2 minutes, beating constantly. Do not allow it to boil.
- Remove pan from heat and ladle soup into serving bowls. Serve immediately, garnished with chopped spring onions.

egg-drop soup

A light, fragrant soup, this classic Egg-drop Soup is adapted from a Cantonese recipe.

Serves 6

Ingredients

Cooking oil	1 Tbsp
Onion	1, medium-sized, peeled and finely sliced
Chicken stock	2 litres (64 fl oz / 8 cups)
Tomatoes	4, medium-sized, quartered
Egg	1, lightly beaten

Method

• In a large saucepan, heat oil over moderate heat. Add onion and cook, stirring constantly, for 1 minute.

• Stir in chicken stock and bring to the boil. Reduce heat to low and simmer, stirring occasionally for 10 minutes.

• Add tomatoes and simmer for a further 5 minutes. Remove pan from heat and beat egg into soup. Ladle into bowls and serve immediately.

moroccan chicken harira

The lentils and rice used in this soup make it substantial, and the spices and lemon juice add a wonderful flavour.

Serves 6–8

Ingredients

Olive oil	3 Tbsp
Chicken	1, small, about 800 g (1³/₄ lb), cut into joints
Onions	2, peeled and finely chopped
Garlic	2 cloves, peeled and crushed
Ground turmeric	¹/₂ tsp
Ground ginger	¹/₂ tsp
Coriander seeds	¹/₂ tsp
Ground cinnamon	¹/₂ tsp
Chicken stock	2 litres (64 fl oz / 8 cups)
Ripe tomatoes	450 g (1 lb), cut into wedges
Split yellow lentils	100 g (3¹/₂ oz), soaked for 1 hour, then drained
Salt	¹/₂ tsp
Ground white pepper	¹/₄ tsp
Chopped fresh parsley	3 Tbsp
Long-grain rice	50 g (2 oz)
Eggs	2, beaten
Lemons	3, 1 squeezed for juice and 2 cut into wedges

Method

- Heat oil in a large pan and brown chicken on all sides. Fry in batches if necessary. Remove chicken and set aside.

- In the same pan, use remaining oil to cook onions and garlic for 5 minutes or until soft, stirring occasionally.

- Return chicken to pan and add turmeric, ginger, coriander and cinnamon. Stir-fry over high heat, then add stock, tomatoes, lentils, salt and pepper. Bring to the boil, then cover. Reduce heat and simmer for 40 minutes.

- Remove chicken from pan and shred meat, discarding skin and bones. Return meat to pan.

- Add 2 Tbsp chopped parsley and rice. Bring to the boil. Reduce heat to simmer and cook for a further 20 minutes or until rice is tender.

- Combine eggs and lemon juice. Slowly pour mixture into soup, whisking constantly.

- Serve immediately, garnished with remaining parsley. Provide lemon wedges on the side for squeezing into soup.

eggs flamenco

This is a delicious way of serving eggs, as a first course or as a light snack.

Serves 4

Ingredients

Olive oil	4 Tbsp
Onion	1, medium-sized, peeled and finely sliced
Garlic	2 cloves, peeled and crushed
Lean bacon	230 g (8 oz), sliced
Red capsicums (bell peppers)	2, small, white pith removed, seeded and chopped
Tomatoes	6, medium-sized, blanched, peeled and finely sliced
White button mushrooms	115 g (4 oz), wiped and finely sliced
Salt	1/2 tsp
Ground black pepper	1/4 tsp
Cayenne pepper	a dash
Dried parsley	1 Tbsp
Canned corn kernels	230 g (8 oz), drained
Eggs	4, large

Method

- Preheat oven to 180°C (350°F).
- Heat oil over moderate heat and cook onion and garlic, stirring occasionally, for 5–7 minutes or until onion is soft but not brown.
- Add bacon and capsicums and stir-fry for 10–12 minutes or until capsicums are soft.
- Stir in tomatoes, mushrooms, salt, pepper, cayenne and parsley. Continue cooking for 5 minutes or until tomatoes begin to pulp.
- Stir in corn kernels and remove from heat.
- Pour mixture into an ovenproof baking dish. Using the back of a spoon, make 4 small depressions in mixture. Break an egg into each depression.
- Place baking dish in the oven and bake for 25–30 minutes or until eggs are set. Serve hot.

steamed egg wrapped in banana leaf

In many parts of Asia, food is cooked in leaves not only because they are readily available, but also because of the amazing fragrance they impart to the cooked food. Here, the fragrance of the banana leaves and spices all combine to create a mouthwatering dish.

Makes 10 parcels

Ingredients

Eggs	8
Salt	$1/2$ tsp
Ground white pepper	$1/2$ tsp
Coconut milk	4 Tbsp

Spices

Red chillies	8
Shallots	5, peeled and chopped
Tomatoes	2, chopped
Candlenuts	3, toasted and crushed
Galangal	3-cm (1$1/2$-in) knob, peeled and chopped
Turmeric	1-cm ($1/2$-in) knob, peeled and chopped
Dried prawn (shrimp) paste (*belacan*)	1 tsp
Lemon grass	5-cm (2-in) length, chopped
Salt	to taste
Sugar	to taste
Banana leaves	10 sheets, each 20 x 20-cm (8 x 8-in)
Bamboo skewers	20

Method

- Beat eggs with salt and pepper and pour into a steaming tray.
- Steam over rapidly boiling water for 15 minutes until set. Allow to cool, then cut into cubes.
- Remove seeds from chillies using gloved hands if a less spicy dish is preferred. Combine spices in a blender and grind into a paste.
- Divide paste into 10 portions. Spoon each portion onto the centre of a banana leaf. Spread paste out a little and top with some egg cubes.
- Fold one-third of banana leaf, along the grain, down over paste, then fold up remaining leaf. Secure open ends with bamboo skewers. Repeat to make 10 parcels.
- Steam parcels over rapidly boiling water for 15 minutes. Remove from heat and serve hot or at room temperature.

egg salad

This unusual and attractive salad may be served with a light fish dish or by itself with hot crusty bread.

Serves 2–4

Ingredients

Hard-boiled eggs	6, shelled and sliced
Green capsicums (bell peppers)	2, small, white pith removed, seeded and chopped
Red capsicum (bell pepper)	1, small, white pith removed, seeded and chopped
White button mushrooms	3, wiped and thinly sliced
Black olives	6, pitted
Chopped walnuts	1 Tbsp

Dressing

Garlic	1 small clove, peeled and crushed
Paprika	1 tsp
White wine vinegar	2 Tbsp
Olive oil	90 ml (3 fl oz / 6 Tbsp)
Salt	$\frac{1}{4}$ tsp
Ground black pepper	a dash
Sugar	$\frac{1}{2}$ tsp

Method

- Arrange eggs, capsicums, mushrooms and olives on a medium-sized serving dish. Sprinkle walnuts over.
- In a screw-top jar, combine ingredients for dressing. Shake briskly and pour dressing over salad. Toss to coat ingredients well with dressing. Refrigerate for at least 30 minutes before serving.

NOTE

Tossing the sliced hard-boiled eggs will probably cause the egg yolks to break apart, which could spoil the look of the dish. For better presentation, serve the salad untossed and toss it just before eating.

egg puffs

These airy Mexican-style egg puffs are subtly flavoured with chilli and oregano. They are great served hot.

Makes 15

Ingredients

Eggs	3, whites and yolks separated
Plain (all-purpose) flour	1 Tbsp
Salt	1/2 tsp
Chilli powder	1/4 tsp
Baking powder	1/2 tsp
Dried oregano	1 tsp
Cooking oil for deep-frying	

Method

- Beat egg whites until stiff peaks form.
- In a separate bowl, beat egg yolks until thick and pale.
- Fold egg whites into yolks, then add flour, salt, chilli powder, baking powder and oregano.
- Heat oil for deep-frying until it is about 180°C (350°F).
- Drop tablespoonfuls of mixture, about 4 at a time, into oil. Fry for 1 minute 30 seconds on each side or until puffs are golden brown.
- With a slotted spoon, remove puffs from oil and drain on absorbent paper. Serve immediately with a chilli sauce of your choice.

eggs in a savoury nest

A filling appetiser or light lunch meal, this should be served hot, straight from the oven.

Serves 4

Ingredients

Butter	45 g (1½ oz)
Onion	1, medium-sized, peeled and finely chopped
Ham	8 slices, cut into squares
Tomatoes	8, medium-sized, blanched, peeled, seeded and chopped
Salt	½ tsp
Freshly ground black pepper	¼ tsp
Dried sage	½ tsp
Cooked long-grain rice	280 g (10 oz)
Eggs	8
Grated Mozzarella cheese	85 g (3 oz)

Method

• Preheat oven to 190°C (375°F).

• In a large pan, heat two-thirds of butter over moderate heat. When foam subsides, add onion and ham. Cook, stirring, until onion is soft and ham golden brown.

• Add tomatoes, salt, pepper and sage and cook for a further 3 minutes. Stir in rice and remove from heat.

• Grease 8 small ramekins or individual ovenproof dishes with remaining butter. Divide rice mixture evenly among them, then break an egg on top of each and sprinkle cheese over.

• Bake for 15 minutes or until egg is cooked and cheese is lightly browned.

• Remove from oven and serve immediately.

egg and sardine hors d'oeuvre

A delicious and very simple hors d'oeuvre, these stuffed eggs may be served with brown bread and butter.

Serves 6

Ingredients

Hard-boiled eggs	6, shelled
Canned sardines	170 g (5½ oz), drained
Mayonnaise	4 Tbsp
Lemon juice	1 Tbsp
Chopped fresh parsley	1 Tbsp
Salt	½ tsp
Ground white pepper	¼ tsp

Method

- Halve eggs lengthwise, then cut a thin slice off the bottom of each half so it has a flat surface to sit on and will not wobble.
- Remove yolks and press them through a strainer into a small bowl.
- Mash sardines into egg yolks. Add mayonnaise, lemon juice, parsley, salt and pepper. Mix well.
- Spoon mixture into prepared whites and serve chilled.

For a variation to this recipe, use cooked and chopped chicken meat instead of sardines, and omit the lemon juice.

eggs stuffed with ham and herbs

Hard-boiled eggs stuffed with a delicious ham and egg mixture and then fried.

Serves 2

Ingredients

Hard-boiled eggs	4, shelled
Ham	55 g (2 oz), finely chopped
Butter	115 g (4 oz)
Chopped fresh chives	1 Tbsp
Dried thyme	1 tsp
Worcestershire sauce	1 tsp
Eggs	2
Salt	$\frac{1}{2}$ tsp
Ground black pepper	$\frac{1}{4}$ tsp
Dried white breadcrumbs	4 Tbsp

Method

- Cut eggs in half lengthwise. Remove yolks and place in a mixing bowl. Set whites aside.
- Add ham, half the butter, chives, thyme, Worcestershire sauce, 1 egg, salt and pepper to egg yolks. With a wooden spoon, cream mixture thoroughly until smooth.
- Spoon mixture into egg white halves. Sandwich halves together to form a whole egg. The halves should not fit tightly together.
- In a small bowl, lightly beat remaining raw egg with a fork. Roll stuffed eggs in beaten egg, then roll in breadcrumbs.
- In a pan, melt remaining butter over moderate heat. Place stuffed, coated eggs in pan and fry for 5 minutes or until eggs are golden brown all over.
- With a slotted spoon, carefully transfer stuffed eggs from pan to a warmed serving dish. Serve immediately.

eggs with sherry

Soft-boiled eggs and bacon on toast in a creamy, sherry-and-cheese flavoured sauce.

Serves 4

Ingredients

Butter	30 g (1 oz)
Plain (all-purpose) flour	1 Tbsp
Milk	190 ml (6 fl oz / ¾ cup)
Double (heavy) cream	190 ml (6 fl oz / ¾ cup)
Salt	½ tsp
Ground white pepper	¼ tsp
Cheddar cheese	55 g (2 oz), grated
Dry sherry	4 Tbsp
Egg yolks	2, lightly beaten
Crusty bread	4 slices, toasted and buttered
Bacon rashers	4, crisp-fried
Eggs	4, fried sunny side up or soft-boiled
Paprika	1 tsp

Method

- In a pan, melt butter over moderate heat. Remove pan from heat and, with a wooden spoon, stir in flour to make a smooth paste. Gradually add milk and cream, stirring constantly.

- Return pan to heat. Add salt and pepper. Cook, stirring constantly, for 2–3 minutes or until sauce thickens.

- Stir in cheese and sherry. Continue cooking and stirring until cheese melts. Remove pan from heat and beat in egg yolks. Set aside.

- Top each slice of toast with bacon and a sunny side up. If using soft-boiled eggs, crack one over each serving. Spoon sauce over, sprinkle with paprika and serve immediately.

eggs with tomatoes and onion

This is a simple but very tasty dish. It may be served on its own or with a side dish of steamed corn kernels.

Serves 2

Ingredients

Olive oil	2 Tbsp
Onion	1, small, peeled and finely chopped
Garlic	1 clove, peeled and crushed
Tomatoes	6, thinly sliced
Salt	1/2 tsp
Dried basil	1/4 tsp
Cayenne pepper	a dash
Crusty bread	2 large slices, toasted and buttered
Poached eggs	4
Grated Parmesan cheese	2 Tbsp

Method

- In a pan, heat oil over moderate heat. Add onion and garlic and fry for 5–7 minutes or until onion is soft and translucent but not brown.
- Add tomatoes, salt, basil and cayenne. Continue cooking, stirring frequently, for a further 5 minutes.
- Remove pan from heat. Spoon tomato-and-onion mixture onto slices of toast. Place 2 poached eggs on top of each slice and sprinkle with Parmesan cheese. Serve immediately.

If using smaller slices of bread, use four slices instead of two, and top each slice with just one poached egg.

egg tartlets

These decorative tartlets are great for parties as their components—pastry cases, mayonnaise and hard-boiled eggs—can be made well in advance and assembled before serving.

Serves 6

Ingredients

Hard-boiled eggs	4, shelled and finely chopped

Pastry

Plain (all-purpose) flour	170 g (6 oz)
Salt	a dash
Butter	60 g (2 oz), cut into cubes
Vegetable shortening	45 g (1½ oz), cut into cubes
Cold water	1–2 Tbsp

Mayonnaise

Egg yolks	2, at room temperature
Salt	½ tsp
Ground white pepper	a dash
Olive oil	250 ml (8 fl oz / 1 cup)
Lemon juice or white wine vinegar	1 Tbsp
Garlic	1 large clove, peeled and crushed
Chopped basil	4 Tbsp

Garnish

Hard-boiled egg	6 slices
Basil	6 small sprigs

Method

- Preheat oven to 200°C (400°F).

- Prepare pastry. Sift flour and salt into a mixing bowl. Add 45 g (1½ oz) butter and shortening, then rub fat into flour until mixture resembles fine breadcrumbs.

- Add 1 Tbsp cold water to flour mixture and knead dough until smooth. Add more cold water if dough is too dry. Refrigerate for 30 minutes.

- Use remaining butter to grease 6 tartlet tins, each 7.5-cm (3-in) in diameter.

- Prepare mayonnaise. Whisk egg yolks, salt and pepper until well blended. Add oil, a few drops at a time, whisking constantly. Do not add oil too quickly or mixture will curdle. When it has thickened, oil may be added more rapidly.

- Beat in a few drops of lemon juice or vinegar from time to time to prevent mayonnaise from becoming too thick. When all the oil has been added, stir in remaining lemon juice or vinegar. Stir in garlic and basil.

- On a lightly floured surface, roll out chilled dough to 0.5-cm (¼-in) thickness. Using a 10-cm (4-in) round pastry cutter, cut out 6 circles and line tartlet tins, trimming off any excess.

- Fill pastry shells with crumpled greaseproof paper and bake blind for 15 minutes, removing paper 5 minutes before to allow pastry to brown. Remove from oven and leave to cool for 30 minutes before turning pastry out of tins.

- Half-fill pastry shells with hard-boiled eggs, then spoon mayonnaise over. Garnish each tartlet with a slice of hard-boiled egg and a sprig of basil. Serve.

eggs three ways

These simple dishes make convenient starters or appetisers for a Chinese meal.

Serves 4

Ingredients

Century Egg and Preserved Ginger

Century eggs	2
Preserved ginger slices	

Bean Sprouts with Egg

Bean sprouts	150 g
Cooking oil	2 tsp
Chopped garlic	1/2 tsp
Salt	to taste
Ground white pepper	to taste
Egg	1, lightly beaten

Quail Eggs

Quail eggs	8, hard-boiled and shelled
Egg	1, lightly beaten
Dried white breadcrumbs	2 Tbsp
Cooking oil	4 Tbsp

Method

- Scrape paste off century eggs, then wash eggs well. Shell eggs and cut into wedges. Place on a serving dish together with slices of preserved ginger. Set aside.
- Wash bean sprouts and pluck off tails if desired.
- Heat oil in a wok and stir-fry garlic until fragrant. Add bean sprouts and lightly stir-fry for 30 seconds. Sprinkle in salt and pepper to taste.
- Pour egg over bean sprouts and lightly stir-fry to scramble mixture. Remove from wok when egg is cooked. Transfer to a serving dish.
- Roll quail eggs in beaten egg, then roll in breadcrumbs.
- Heat oil over moderate heat. Lower coated quail eggs into oil and fry for about 3 minutes or until eggs are golden brown.
- With a slotted spoon, carefully transfer eggs to a serving dish. Serve immediately with other 2 dishes.

scrambled eggs in pastry shells

A delicious and light but filling starter for a dinner party. Follow it up with a light main dish such as grilled (broiled) fish or meat.

Serves 5

Ingredients

Frozen puff pastry	1 small pack
Eggs	6 + 1, lightly beaten
Milk	4 Tbsp
Ground nutmeg	$\frac{1}{4}$ tsp
Salt	$\frac{1}{2}$ tsp
Ground white pepper	$\frac{1}{2}$ tsp
Chopped fresh parsley	1 Tbsp
Chopped fresh chives	1 tsp
Grated Parmesan cheese	2 Tbsp
Butter	1 tsp

Method

- Thaw puff pastry according to manufacturer's instructions. Roll puff pastry out into a 0.5-cm ($\frac{1}{4}$-in) thick sheet.

- Using a 5-cm (2-in) round cutter, cut 20 rounds from puff pastry sheet. Using a 3-cm (1$\frac{1}{2}$-in) round cutter, cut 10 pastry rounds to form rings. Discard smaller rounds.

- Brush complete rounds with beaten egg and place a ring on top of each one. Transfer to a baking tray and brush pastry with remaining beaten egg.

- Bake in a preheated oven at 180°C (350°F) for 5–7 minutes or until pastry has risen and is golden brown. Remove from tray and allow to cool.

- Combine eggs, milk, nutmeg, salt, pepper, parsley, chives and Parmesan, then whisk for 2 minutes or until ingredients are thoroughly blended.

- Melt butter in a pan over low heat. Add egg mixture and cook, stirring constantly, until it is soft and scrambled.

- Fill each pastry shell with a generous portion of scrambled egg mixture and serve immediately.

 NOTE

For greater convenience, you may use ready-rolled puff pastry sheets, but as they are thinner, the pastry shells will not rise as much when baked.

Enjoy the cooler ~~~~~~ by spend~~~~
~~~~~~ with friends in the great outd~~~
~~~~~~ with crisp, fresh air ...

poultry

eggs creole

A tasty way to use up leftover meat, Eggs Creole can also be made with lamb, beef or pork. Serve, as is traditional with Creole dishes, on a bed of plain rice.

Serves 4

Ingredients

Eggs	6, lightly beaten
Salt	½ tsp
Ground black pepper	¼ tsp
Grated nutmeg	a dash
Milk	2 Tbsp
Butter	30 g (1 oz)
Onion	1, peeled and finely chopped
Tomatoes	4, large, blanched, peeled and chopped, or use 400 g (14 oz) canned, peeled tomatoes, drained and chopped
Red capsicum (bell pepper)	1, small, white pith removed, seeded and chopped
Cayenne pepper	a dash
Cooked chicken meat	230 g (7½ oz), finely diced

Method

- In a mixing bowl, beat eggs, salt, pepper, nutmeg and milk together with a fork until ingredients are well blended. Set aside.

- In a pan, heat butter over moderate heat. When foam subsides, add onion, tomatoes, capsicum and cayenne pepper. Cook, stirring occasionally, for 5 minutes or until onion and capsicum are soft but not brown.

- Add chicken and continue cooking for 5 minutes.

- Reduce heat to low and stir in egg mixture. Cook, stirring constantly, until eggs are scrambled.

- Transfer mixture to a serving dish and serve immediately.

eggs baked with chicken and tomatoes

This dish offers a tasty way of using up leftover chicken. Alternatively, diced ham may be substituted for the chicken.

Serves 6

Ingredients

Butter	1 Tbsp
Tomatoes	2, sliced
Cooked chicken meat	115 g (4 oz), finely chopped
Eggs	6
Salt	½ tsp
Ground black pepper	¼ tsp
Paprika	1 tsp

Method

- Preheat oven to 180°C (350°F).
- Grease 6 ramekins with butter. Put a slice of tomato into each one, then spoon some chicken meat on top. Break an egg into each dish and sprinkle with salt and pepper.
- Cover dishes with buttered greaseproof paper and stand dishes in a baking tin of hot water.
- Place tin in the oven and bake for 10 minutes.
- Remove dishes from oven and sprinkle paprika over. Serve immediately.

Prepare this dish in glass ramekins if possible, as the colour of the tomato, egg white and egg yolk will show through the glass, making this dish visually very appealing.

egg rolls

The completed dish looks very impressive, with the different layers of yellow, black and white colours. It can be served as part of a meal or as finger food.

Serves 4–6

Ingredients

Minced chicken	120 g (4 oz)
Salt	1/2 tsp
Chinese cooking wine (*hua tiao*)	2 tsp
Chopped ginger	1/2 tsp
Black moss (*fa cai*)	50 g (2 oz), soaked, drained and finely chopped
Egg white	1
Eggs	4, beaten
Corn flour (cornstarch)	1 Tbsp, mixed with 1 1/2 Tbsp water

Method

- Mix minced chicken with salt, wine, ginger, black moss and egg white. Set aside.
- Steam half the beaten eggs on a 12–15-cm (5–6-in) wide plate for 5 minutes or until set. Set aside to cool before cutting into long, thick strips.
- Add corn flour to remaining beaten eggs and make 2 thin omelettes.
- Spread half the minced chicken mixture over an omelette. Place a strip of steamed egg in the middle and roll omelette up. Repeat with other omelette.
- Transfer rolls to a steaming plate; make sure each one is resting on open flap. Steam for 8 minutes.
- Remove rolls from heat and cut into 1-cm (1/2-in) thick slices. Serve hot.

eggah with noodles and chicken

An eggah is an Arab-style omelette. It is firm and thick, rather like an egg cake. It can be cut into wedges and served as a main dish or into small pieces and served as an appetiser.

Serves 6

Ingredients

Water	1.5 litres (48 fl oz / 6 cups)
Salt	1$\frac{1}{2}$ tsp
Egg noodles	115 g (4 oz)
Eggs	6
Ground black pepper	$\frac{1}{2}$ tsp
Cayenne pepper	$\frac{1}{8}$–$\frac{1}{4}$ tsp
Paprika	2 tsp
Ground cumin	1 tsp
Garlic	1 clove, peeled and crushed
Cooked chicken meat	230 g (7$\frac{1}{2}$ oz), diced
Butter	55 g (2 oz)

Method

- Pour water into a large saucepan over high heat. Add ½ tsp salt and bring to the boil.
- Add noodles and cover pan. Reduce heat to low and simmer, stirring occasionally, for 6–8 minutes or until noodles are cooked. Remove pan from heat. Drain noodles and set aside. Discard water.
- In a mixing bowl, beat eggs, remaining salt, pepper, spices and garlic together with a wire whisk until mixture is light and frothy. Stir in chicken and noodles.
- In a large pan, melt butter over moderate heat. When foam subsides, reduce heat to low and pour in egg mixture. Cook slowly for 20–30 minutes or until underside is golden brown and eggah is cooked through.
- Remove pan from heat and place under a preheated grill set on high for 5 minutes or until top of eggah is golden brown.
- Serve hot, cut into wedges.

ukrainian chicken kiev

These butter-stuffed, deep-fried chicken breasts are a Russian restaurant classic. They are surprisingly easy to prepare.

Serves 6

Ingredients

Butter	175 g (6 oz)
Lemon	1, grated for zest and squeezed for juice
Garlic	2 cloves, peeled and crushed
Chopped chives	3 Tbsp
Chicken breasts	6 large pieces, boned and skinned
Salt	½ tsp
Ground black pepper	½ tsp
Cooking oil for deep-frying	
Eggs	2, beaten
Dried white breadcrumbs	175 g (6 oz)

Method

- Mash butter with lemon zest and juice, garlic and chives. Mould mixture into a rectangle, wrap in foil and refrigerate.

- Lay chicken breasts between 2 sheets of plastic wrap and pound them flat with a rolling pin or meat mallet. Remove plastic wrap and season chicken with salt and pepper.

- Working quickly, cut chilled butter into 6 fingers and place one along the centre of each fillet. Fold chicken tightly over butter to enclose completely. Wrap each chicken parcel in plastic wrap and freeze for 20–30 minutes.

- Heat oil for deep-frying in a large pan.

- Remove chicken parcels from freezer and unwrap.

- Dip chicken parcels into beaten egg, allowing excess to drip back into bowl, then coat with breadcrumbs. Firmly press in breadcrumbs so coating is secure.

- Lower 2–3 parcels into hot oil, depending on the size of pan and fry for 5–6 minutes or until golden brown. Remove and drain on absorbent paper. Repeat to cook remaining parcels.

- Serve hot.

crunchy chicken and corn fritters

These corn fritters go well with deep-fried chicken, but they make a tasty snack on their own as well.

Serves 4–6

Ingredients

Plain (all-purpose) flour	125 g (4½ oz)
Salt	¼ tsp
Eggs	2
Milk	180 ml (6 fl oz / ¾ cup)
Chicken	150 g (5 oz), cut into small cubes
Corn kernels	175 g (6 oz)
Green capsicum (bell pepper)	1, white pith removed, seeded and finely chopped
Cooking oil for pan-frying	

Method

- Sift flour and salt together into a bowl. Make a well in the centre and add eggs.
- Gradually add milk, drawing flour in from sides of bowl. Mix until a smooth, creamy batter is achieved.
- Stir in chicken, corn kernels and capsicum. Leave to stand for about 30 minutes.
- Take a large pan and add enough oil to cover cooking surface. Heat until smoking, then add 3–4 spoonfuls of batter, depending on size of pan. Fry for about 2 minutes or until golden brown and puffy around the edges. Turn over to fry other side.
- Remove fritters and drain on absorbent paper. Repeat with remaining batter until used up. Serve hot.

lacy egg pancakes with chicken curry

This is a dish of Malay origin. A cup with 4–5 small spouts is used to make this pancake, but using your fingers will do as well. These pancakes are ideal eaten with chicken curry.

Serves 4–6

Ingredients

Chicken Curry

Chicken	1, about 800 g (1³⁄₄ lb), cut into pieces
Chicken curry powder	3 Tbsp
Garlic	4 cloves, peeled and chopped
Salt	1 tsp
Cooking oil	2 Tbsp
Shallots	4, peeled and sliced
Curry leaves	1 sprig, stem discarded
Coconut milk	750 ml (24 fl oz / 3 cups)

Lacy Pancakes

Plain (all-purpose) flour	250 g (8¹⁄₂ oz), sifted
Salt	¹⁄₂ tsp
Eggs	2, beaten
Coconut milk	500 ml (16 fl oz / 2 cups)
Yellow food colouring	2–3 drops
Cooking oil	2 Tbsp

Method

- Prepare chicken curry. Season chicken with curry powder, garlic and salt. Leave for 20–30 minutes.

- Heat oil in a pan and fry shallots and curry leaves until shallots are limp. Add chicken and fry to seal in juices.

- Add coconut milk, cover pan and simmer for 30 minutes until chicken is tender.

- Meanwhile, prepare pancakes. Combine flour and salt in a bowl, then stir in eggs, coconut milk and food colouring until batter is smooth. Strain batter if necessary.

- Heat 1 tsp oil in a pan over low heat. Using your fingers, scoop up some batter and let it flow in continuous streams onto the pan as you move your hand in a circular motion to create a lacy pattern. This might take a bit of practice. When pancake is set, remove to a plate.

- Repeat to make more pancakes until batter is used up. Fold pancakes as desired and serve hot with chicken curry.

meat

egg and bacon bake

A light dish which may be served with spinach or peas.

Serves 2–4

Ingredients

Butter	45 g (1½ oz)
Plain (all-purpose) flour	2 Tbsp
Milk	315 ml (10½ fl oz / 1¼ cups)
Bay leaf	1
Ground nutmeg	a dash
Lean bacon	230 g (7½ oz), pan-fried and coarsely sliced
Salt	¼ tsp
Ground black pepper	¼ tsp
Tomatoes	4, chopped
Hard-boiled eggs	6, shelled and sliced
Egg	1, lightly beaten

Topping

Dried white breadcrumbs	85 g (3 oz)
Butter	45 g (1½ oz), cut into small cubes

Method

- Preheat oven to 190°C (375°F).

- In a saucepan, melt two-thirds of butter over moderate heat. Remove pan from heat and, with a wooden spoon, stir in flour to make a smooth paste. Gradually add milk, stirring constantly.

- Return pan to heat and add bay leaf and nutmeg. Bring mixture to the boil, still stirring. Reduce heat to low and cook for 2–3 minutes or until sauce is thick and smooth.

- Remove pan from heat. Discard bay leaf. Stir in bacon, salt, pepper and tomatoes.

- Grease a baking dish with remaining butter, then line with hard-boiled egg slices.

- Stir beaten egg into sauce in pan and pour over egg slices in baking dish.

- Add topping ingredients. Sprinkle breadcrumbs on top and dot with butter.

- Bake for 40 minutes. Serve hot.

egg and bacon scramble

Serve this as a light lunch dish or as a hot hors d'oeuvre.
Serves 4

Ingredients

Cooking oil	1 Tbsp
Onion	1, medium-sized, peeled and finely chopped
Streaky bacon	8 rashers, coarsely chopped
Courgettes (zucchini)	4, ends discarded and chopped
White button mushrooms	115 g (4 oz), wiped clean and halved
Salt	½ tsp
Ground black pepper	¼ tsp
Eggs	6
Milk	4 Tbsp
Grated nutmeg	a dash
Dried white breadcrumbs	55 g (2 oz)
Butter	1 Tbsp, cut into small cubes

Method

- Heat oil in a pan over moderate heat. Add onion and bacon and cook, stirring occasionally, for 5–7 minutes or until onion is soft but not brown and bacon is cooked.

- Add courgettes, mushrooms, salt and pepper. Reduce heat to low and cook, stirring occasionally, for 15 minutes or until courgettes are tender. Remove pan from heat and set aside.

- Preheat grill (broiler) to high.

- In a mixing bowl, beat eggs, milk and nutmeg together, then stir mixture into pan's contents.

- Return pan to heat and cook gently, stirring constantly, until eggs are nearly scrambled. Remove from heat.

- Pour egg mixture into a deep heatproof (flameproof) dish. Sprinkle breadcrumbs over and dot with butter.

- Place dish under grill for 3 minutes or until top is lightly browned. Remove from heat and serve immediately.

egg white with corn, peas and sausage

This recipe comes in handy when you have leftover egg whites from baking. Although egg white is bland on its own, the combination of corn kernels, peas, sausage and flavourful sauce makes this dish both colourful and tasty.

Serves 3–4

Ingredients

Green peas	55 g (2 oz)
Corn kernels	70 g (2¹/₂ oz)
Chicken sausage	1, diced
Egg whites	5, lightly beaten
Cooking oil for deep-frying	
Salt	to taste
Ground white pepper	to taste

Sauce

Finely grated ginger	1 tsp
Chinese cooking wine (*hua tiao*)	1 tsp
Sugar	¹/₂ tsp
Corn flour (cornstarch)	1 tsp, mixed with 100 ml (3¹/₂ oz) water
Sesame oil	1 tsp

Method

- Mix peas, corn and diced sausage with egg whites.
- Heat oil for deep-frying in a wok. Slowly pour in egg white mixture and deep-fry until set.
- Use a strainer to remove fried egg mixture from wok. Drain well and place on a serving plate.
- Remove oil, leaving 1 Tbsp oil in wok, and prepare sauce. Add ginger and fry until fragrant.
- Stir in remaining ingredients and simmer until slightly thick.
- Pour sauce over fried egg mixture and serve.

egg burgers

Egg burgers are especially popular with children. They make a delicious snack, but can also be served as a light meal. Allow 2 burgers per person.

Serves 2

Ingredients

Soft burger buns	2, halved lengthways
Butter	55 g (2 oz)
Ham	2 round slices
Prepared mustard	2 tsp
Cheddar cheese	4 slices
Cooking oil	2 Tbsp
Eggs	2

Method

- Preheat grill (broiler) to high, then lightly toast cut sides of buns until golden brown. Remove from heat. Keep grill hot.

- Spread each toasted bun half with butter, then top each bottom half with ham. Spread a little mustard over each slice of ham and cover with a slice of cheese.

- Place bun halves under hot grill for 5 minutes or until cheese has melted and turned golden brown.

- While buns are bring grilled, heat oil in a pan over moderate heat and fry eggs sunny side up or until whites are solid and yolks still runny and soft.

- Remove buns from grill and place a fried egg on each one. Top with remaining bun halves. Serve immediately.

As a variation to this burger recipe, use hamburger patties or bacon rashers instead of sliced ham.

eggs essen

A delicious combination of capsicum, onion, tomatoes, frankfurters and eggs, Eggs Essen is a colourful and substantial meal in itself.

Serves 4–6

Ingredients

Olive oil	4 Tbsp
Onion	1, medium-sized, peeled and finely chopped
Potatoes	2, medium-sized, peeled and diced
Ham	55 g (2 oz), sliced
Green capsicum (bell pepper)	1, small, white pith removed, seeded and finely chopped
Canned peeled tomatoes	230 g (7½ oz), drained and chopped
Frankfurters	8, cut into 1-cm (½-in) slices
Dried basil	¼ tsp
Eggs	6
Salt	1 tsp
Ground black pepper	½ tsp

Method

- Preheat oven to 230°C (450°F).

- In a pan, heat oil over moderate heat. Add onion and potatoes and cook, stirring occasionally, for 5 minutes.

- Add ham, capsicum, tomatoes, frankfurters and basil. Cook, stirring occasionally, for 15 minutes.

- Remove pan from heat and transfer mixture into a medium-sized ovenproof dish. Smooth surface with a knife.

- Break eggs on top of mixture and sprinkle with salt and pepper.

- Place dish in oven and bake for 8–10 minutes or until egg whites are set.

- Remove from oven and serve immediately.

egg foo yong

A Chinese omelette, Egg Foo Yong is a crunchy combination of eggs, ham and bean sprouts. Serve it as part of a Chinese meal.

Serves 2

Ingredients

Eggs	4
Light soy sauce	1 Tbsp
Salt	½ tsp
Ground black pepper	¼ tsp
Butter	30 g (1 oz)
Shallot	1, peeled and finely chopped
Bean sprouts	115 g (4 oz)
Ham	55 g (2 oz), cut into thin strips
Chopped spring onion (scallion)	2 tsp

Method

- In a mixing bowl, beat eggs, soy sauce, salt and pepper together until mixture is light and fluffy. Set aside.

- In a medium-sized pan, melt butter over moderate heat. When foam subsides, add shallot, bean sprouts and ham. Fry for 4–5 minutes, stirring occasionally.

- Pour beaten egg mixture into pan. Stir with a fork and leave to set.

- Transfer omelette to a serving plate, garnish with spring onions and serve immediately.

NOTE

The omelette will vary in thickness depending on the size of the pan used. Use a smaller pan if a thicker omelette is preferred. This will however require a longer cooking time.

steamed egg with minced meat

This is a very simple but tasty and nutritious dish that goes well with plain rice.

Serves 2–3

Ingredients

Large eggs	3
Salt	1 tsp
Light soy sauce	1 Tbsp
Ground white pepper	to taste
Water	300 ml (10 fl oz / 1¼ cups)
Minced meat	150 g (5 oz)
Salted egg yolk	1, cut into small pieces
Century egg	1, shelled and cut into small pieces
Spring onion (scallion)	1, chopped

Method

• Beat eggs and stir in salt, soy sauce, pepper and water.

• Add minced meat, salted egg yolk and century egg, ensuring that meat is not in clumps.

• Pour mixture into a steaming dish and steam over rapidly boiling water for 12–15 minutes or until eggs are set and meat is cooked.

• Remove from heat and serve hot with plain rice.

NOTE

This recipe will still turn out without the addition of salted egg and/or century egg, if you prefer to omit them, or if they are not available. The two types of egg add extra flavour to the dish.

egyptian braised steak

Egyptian Braised Steak, with chickpeas and eggs cooked in their shells, makes a rich, satisfying meal. It is left to cook for a long time, and so combines superlative flavour with convenience.

Serves 6

Ingredients

Cooking oil	3 Tbsp
Onions	2, large, peeled and chopped
Stewing steak	900 g (2 lb), cut into 2.5-cm (1-in) cubes
Potatoes	2, large, peeled and diced
Eggs	6, shells thoroughly cleaned
Chickpeas	330 g (12 oz), soaked overnight and drained
Garlic	1 clove, peeled and crushed
Ground turmeric	1 tsp
Ground cumin	½ tsp
Salt	1½ tsp
Ground black pepper	1 tsp
Beef stock	2 Tbsp, made by dissolving 1 beef stock cube in 2 Tbsp boiling water

Method

- In a medium-sized pan, heat oil over moderate heat. Add onions and fry for 5–7 minutes or until onions are soft and translucent but not brown.

- Add meat and cook, stirring occasionally, for 10 minutes or until meat is brown.

- Remove pan from heat and transfer onions, meat and oil to a large pot.

- Add all remaining ingredients and pour in enough water to cover them.

- Cover pot and simmer over low heat for 2–3 hours until meat is tender. Serve hot with rice or bread.

baked eggs with cheese

A tasty and filling dish with a pleasant, mild flavour.

Serves 4

Ingredients

Butter	1 Tbsp
Lean bacon	225 g (7$\frac{1}{2}$ oz), sliced
Sliced white bread	2 slices, crusts removed and discarded, diced
Eggs	8
Salt	$\frac{1}{4}$ tsp
Ground black pepper	a dash
Mozzarella cheese	4 thin slices

Method

- Preheat oven to 190°C (375°F).
- In a small pan, melt butter over moderate heat. When foam subsides, add bacon and bread. Stir-fry for 6–8 minutes or until bacon and bread are crisp and lightly browned. Remove pan from heat.
- Divide bacon and bread equally among 4 small baking dishes, each suited for an individual serving. Break 2 eggs into each dish, then sprinkle salt and pepper over.
- Place a slice of cheese on top of eggs. The cheese will not completely cover eggs but it will spread with cooking.
- Bake dishes for 10–15 minutes or until eggs are just set and cheese has melted and spread.
- Remove dishes from oven and serve immediately. Garnish as desired.

salted and century eggs porridge

This porridge is simple but hearty and amazingly tasty, especially with the addition of salted and century eggs.

Serves 4

Ingredients

Pork loin	100 g (3$\frac{1}{2}$ oz)
Salt	1 Tbsp
Long-grain rice	90 g (3 oz)
Water	1.5 litres (48 fl oz / 6 cups)
Salted egg	1, cleaned and hard-boiled
Century egg	1, cleaned
Chopped spring onion (scallion)	1 Tbsp

Condiments

Light soy sauce
Ground white pepper
Red chilli slices

Method

- Season pork with salt and refrigerate overnight. Rinse pork and pat dry before use.
- In a pot, combine rice, pork and 1 litre water. Bring to the boil for 20 minutes, uncovered.
- Lower heat and remove pork. Mash rice with the back of a ladle until well broken up. This will make the porridge smoother.
- Shred pork and return to pot. Shell salted and century eggs and cut into small pieces. Add to pot.
- Add remaining water to pot and bring to the boil, simmering for another 10–15 minutes or until porridge is smooth.
- Ladle porridge into individual serving bowls. Garnish with chopped spring onions and serve hot. Provide condiments on the side for diners to use as desired.

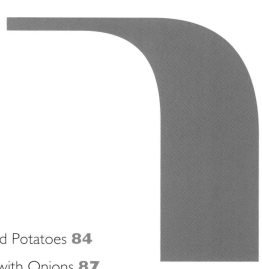

vegetarian

eggs in baked potatoes

These baked potatoes are stuffed with a mixture of eggs, butter, cream and chives, making this delicious and filling dish suitable for a light, casual meal.

Serves 4

Ingredients

Potatoes	4, large, scrubbed and dried
Butter	1 Tbsp
Chopped chives	1 Tbsp
Salt	1 tsp
Ground black pepper	¼ tsp
Grated nutmeg	a dash
Double (heavy) cream	4 Tbsp
Eggs	4

Method

• Preheat oven to 190°C (375°F). Prick potatoes lightly with a fork, then bake for 30 minutes.

• Remove potatoes from oven. Leave oven at 190°C (375°F). Cut about 2.5-cm (1-in) off tops of potatoes. Using a teaspoon, scoop out the inside of each potato, taking care not to tear the skin. Set potato skins aside.

• Place potato in a mixing bowl and mash with butter using a fork or potato masher. Add chives, salt, pepper and nutmeg. Stir in cream and beat until ingredients are thoroughly combined. Gradually beat in eggs.

• Fill each hollowed-out potato with egg and cream mixture and place in a baking dish. Return to oven for 10–12 minutes or until filling is lightly browned on top. Serve immediately.

eggs baked with onions

This is a light and tasty dish that goes well with hot crusty bread and a crisp green salad.

Serves 4

Ingredients

Butter	30 g (1 oz) + 1 tsp
Olive oil	2 Tbsp
Onions	3, medium-sized, peeled and thinly sliced into rings
Hard-boiled eggs	6, shelled and sliced
Salt	1 tsp
Cayenne pepper	a dash
Plain (all-purpose) flour	1 Tbsp
Single (light) cream	250 ml (8 fl oz / 1 cup)
Milk	4 Tbsp
White wine	4 Tbsp
Grated Cheddar cheese	3 Tbsp

Method

- Lightly grease a shallow heatproof (flameproof) dish using 1 tsp butter.
- In a medium-sized pan, heat oil over moderate heat. Add onion rings and fry for 8–10 minutes or until golden brown.
- Remove pan from heat and, with a slotted spoon, transfer half the onions to buttered dish.
- Cover with a layer of hard-boiled eggs, then remaining onions. Sprinkle with salt and cayenne pepper. Set aside.
- Preheat grill (broiler) to high.
- In a small saucepan, melt remaining butter over moderate heat. Remove pan from heat and, with a wooden spoon, stir in flour to make a smooth paste. Gradually add cream, milk and wine, stirring constantly.
- Return pan to heat and stir constantly for 2–3 minutes or until sauce is thick and smooth. Add 2 Tbsp cheese and continue stirring for a further 3 minutes.
- Pour sauce over layered ingredients in dish. Sprinkle remaining cheese on top.
- Place dish under grill (broiler) and cook for about 3 minutes or until cheese is bubbling and golden brown. Serve immediately.

eggs baked with creamed mushrooms

A delicious dish of poached eggs baked with cream, cheese and mushrooms.

Serves 4

Ingredients

Butter	1 Tbsp + $\frac{1}{2}$ tsp
Eggs	4, lightly poached
White button mushrooms	230 g (8 oz), wiped and sliced
Salt	$\frac{1}{2}$ tsp
Ground black pepper	$\frac{1}{4}$ tsp
Cayenne pepper	a dash
Single (light) cream	90 ml (3 fl oz / $\frac{3}{8}$ cup)
Chopped fresh parsley	1 Tbsp
Grated Parmesan cheese	2 Tbsp

Method

- Preheat oven to 180°C (350°F).

- Grease a medium-sized baking dish with $\frac{1}{2}$ tsp butter. Arrange poached eggs in dish and set aside.

- In a small saucepan, melt remaining butter over moderate heat. When foam subsides, add mushrooms, salt, pepper and cayenne pepper. Cook, stirring occasionally, for 4–5 minutes or until mushrooms are cooked. Remove pan from heat.

- Stir cream into saucepan, mixing well with mushrooms and their juices. Stir in parsley.

- Pour mushroom mixture over eggs. Sprinkle cheese on top and bake for 15 minutes or until cheese is lightly browned.

- Remove from oven and serve immediately.

indian-style eggs

Curried eggs are ideal for an impromptu meal since they are quick and easy to prepare. Serve with plain rice.

Serves 4

Ingredients

Raisins	55 g (2 oz)
Butter	55 g (2 oz)
Onions	2, medium, peeled and finely chopped
Garlic	1 clove, peeled and crushed
Green apple	1, small, cored and finely diced
Plain (all-purpose) flour	2 Tbsp
Curry powder	2 tsp
Milk	250 ml (8 fl oz / 1 cup)
Double (heavy) cream	4 Tbsp
Salt	$\frac{1}{2}$ tsp
Ground black pepper	$\frac{1}{4}$ tsp
Hard-boiled eggs	4, shelled
Almond slivers	3 Tbsp, toasted

Method

- Place raisins in a small bowl and add enough boiling water to just cover. Allow to soak for 10 minutes, then drain and set aside.

- Meanwhile, in a medium-sized saucepan, melt butter over moderate heat. When foam subsides, add onions, garlic and apple. Cook, stirring occasionally, for 8 minutes or until onions and apple are soft but not brown.

- Stir in flour and curry powder with a wooden spoon. Cook, stirring, for 3 minutes.

- Remove pan from heat and stir in milk. Return pan to heat and cook, stirring, for 3–4 minutes or until sauce has thickened. Stir in cream, salt and pepper.

- Carefully fold eggs into sauce with a metal spoon. Gently simmer for 4–5 minutes or until eggs are thoroughly heated.

- Remove pan from heat and transfer to a serving dish. Sprinkle raisins and almonds on top and serve with rice.

javanese omelette

Unlike the traditional light, fluffy French omelette, the Javanese version is slightly spicy and is cooked until it is completely set and golden brown.

Serves 2–4

Ingredients

Eggs	6
Cold water	1 Tbsp
Salt	½ tsp
Light soy sauce	1 Tbsp
Brown sugar	1 tsp
Cooking oil	2 Tbsp
Onion	1 small, peeled and finely chopped
Green chillies	2, seeded and finely sliced

Method

- In a mixing bowl, beat eggs, water, salt, soy sauce and brown sugar together until mixture is light and foamy. Set aside.
- In a pan, heat oil over moderate heat. Add onion and chillies. Cook, stirring occasionally, until they are soft but not brown.
- Pour in beaten egg mixture and cook until almost set. Lift edges of setting omelette and tilt pan so any remaining liquid egg flows to the bottom of hot pan to cook.
- When omelette is completely set, continue cooking for 3–5 minutes or until base of omelette is golden brown.
- Remove pan from heat and slide omelette onto a serving plate. Garnish, if desired, with more cut green chillies. Serve immediately.

N O T E

Green chillies are usually not as spicy as red chillies. This recipe specifies that the seeds are removed from the green chillies, making them even less spicy. If the spiciness of this dish is still of concern to you, reduce the amount of chillies used.

egg bread

This beautifully light Egg Bread, or Challah, is traditionally baked for Hebrew Sabbaths and festivals. The original recipe uses poppy seeds but here, they have been replaced with black sesame seeds.

Makes one 900 g (2 lb) loaf

Ingredients

Plain (all-purpose) flour	450 g (1 lb / 4 cups)
Sugar	1 Tbsp
Salt	1½ tsp
Dried instant yeast	1 packet, about 2¼ tsp
Milk	180 ml (6 fl oz / ¾ cup)
Eggs	2, beaten
Cooking oil	1 Tbsp
Butter	½ tsp
Egg yolk	1, beaten with 1 Tbsp cold water
Black sesame or poppy seeds	2 Tbsp

Method

- Sift flour, sugar and salt into a large bowl. Add yeast, milk, eggs and oil. Use your fingers or a spatula to gradually draw the flour into the liquid. Continue mixing until flour is fully incorporated and dough comes away from sides of bowl.

- Cover bowl with a clean, damp cloth and leave in a warm, draught-free place for 1½–2 hours or until dough has risen and almost doubled in bulk.

- Turn dough out of bowl onto a lightly floured surface and knead for 5–8 minutes. Divide dough into 3 ropes, each about 30-cm (12-in) long. Fasten ropes together at one end by pressing together and loosely plait (braid) them together, fastening again at the end.

- Preheat oven to 220°C (425°F).

- Place loaf on a buttered baking tray and cover again with clean cloth. Set aside in a warm place for 2 hours or until loaf has risen and expanded across baking tray.

- With a pastry brush, brush top of loaf with egg yolk glaze and sprinkle sesame or poppy seeds over.

- Bake for 10 minutes, then reduce temperature to 190°C (375°F) and bake for a further 25–30 minutes or until loaf is deep golden brown.

- After removing bread from oven, tip loaf off baking tray and rap underside with your knuckles. It is cooked if it sounds hollow. If not, bake for a further 5–10 minutes.

- Cool loaf on a wire rack before serving.

egg and cheese rissoles

These delicious savoury rissoles make a light meal. They can be accompanied by a green salad.

Serves 2–3

Ingredients

Milk	250 ml (8 fl oz / 1 cup)
Salt	1/2 tsp
Ground black pepper	1/4 tsp
Dried dill	1/4 tsp
Butter	30 g (1 oz)
Plain (all-purpose) flour	2 Tbsp
Grated Cheddar cheese	115 g (4 oz)
Chopped fresh parsley	1 Tbsp
Hard-boiled eggs	5, shelled and chopped
Dried white breadcrumbs	30 g (1 oz)
Cooking oil	2 Tbsp

Method

- In a saucepan, heat milk, salt, pepper and dill over low heat for 5 minutes. Remove pan from heat and set aside to cool to lukewarm.
- In another saucepan, melt butter over moderate heat. Remove pan from heat and, with a wooden spoon, stir in flour to make a smooth paste.
- Gradually add warm milk, stirring constantly. Return pan to moderate heat and add cheese and parsley. Cook, stirring constantly, until sauce becomes very thick and smooth.
- Remove pan from heat and fold in eggs. Allow mixture to cool to room temperature, then refrigerate for 30 minutes.
- Shape mixture into small patties and flatten them slightly. Dip each patty into breadcrumbs so that it is well coated all over.
- In a large pan, heat oil over moderate heat. Add rissoles and fry them for 4 minutes on each side, or until they are golden brown. Drain on absorbent paper and serve hot.

egg and corn savoury

This delicious dish is simple and quick to prepare. Serve it with thick slices of brown bread and butter.

Serves 4

Ingredients

Butter	30 g (1 oz)
Garlic	1 clove, peeled and crushed
Onion	1, medium-sized, peeled and finely sliced
Day-old white bread	4 slices, crusts trimmed, cut into small squares
Canned creamed corn soup	280 ml (10$\frac{1}{2}$ fl oz)
Tomato purée	2 Tbsp
Corn kernels	330 g (11 oz)
Potatoes	420 g (14 oz), peeled and cut into small cubes
Salt	$\frac{1}{2}$ tsp
Ground black pepper	$\frac{1}{2}$–1 tsp
Paprika	1 tsp
Worcestershire sauce	1 Tbsp
Eggs	6
Milk	4 Tbsp

Method

- In a large saucepan, melt butter over moderate heat. When foam subsides, add garlic, onion and bread.
- Cook mixture, stirring occasionally, for 5–7 minutes or until onion is soft and translucent and bread crisp.
- Stir in soup, tomato purée, corn kernels, potatoes, salt, pepper, paprika and Worcestershire sauce. Reduce heat to low and simmer, stirring constantly, for 15 minutes or until potatoes are soft.
- In a small mixing bowl, beat eggs and milk together. Stir mixture into pan.
- Simmer for a further 10 minutes, stirring constantly, or until mixture is thick and creamy. Remove pan from heat and transfer to a serving dish. Serve immediately.

egg and cream cheese tart

This simple tart is excellent for a family weekend lunch.

Makes one 22.5-cm (9-in) tart

Ingredients

Pastry

Plain (all-purpose) flour	170 g (5$\frac{1}{2}$ oz)
Salt	a dash
Butter	45 g (1$\frac{1}{2}$ oz), cut into small cubes
Vegetable shortening	45 g (1$\frac{1}{2}$ oz), cut into small cubes
Cold water	1–2 Tbsp

Filling

Cream cheese	250 g (9 oz)
Double (heavy) cream	125 ml (4 fl oz / $\frac{1}{2}$ cup)
Eggs	6
Spring onions (scallions)	6, finely chopped
Salt	$\frac{1}{2}$ tsp
Ground white pepper	$\frac{1}{4}$ tsp

Method

- Prepare pastry. Sift flour and salt into a mixing bowl. Add butter and vegetable shortening. Rub fat into flour with your fingertips until mixture resembles fine breadcrumbs.

- Add 1 Tbsp cold water and, using a table knife, mix it into flour mixture. Knead dough until it is smooth. Add more water if dough is too dry. Pat dough into a ball, cover with greaseproof paper and refrigerate for 30 minutes.

- Preheat oven to 190°C (375°F).

- Prepare filling. In a mixing bowl, beat cream cheese and cream together with a wooden spoon until mixture is smooth. Beat in eggs, spring onions, salt and pepper.

- On a floured surface, roll out dough into a circle 0.5-cm ($\frac{1}{4}$-in) thick. Lift dough using rolling pin and lay it over a 22.5-cm (9-in) flan tin. Gently ease dough in and trim edges.

- Spoon cream cheese mixture into pastry case, then bake for 30 minutes or until pastry case is golden brown and filling is set. Serve hot.

egg cutlets

A substantial, economic dish, Egg Cutlets may be served with a green vegetable or salad.

Serves 2–4

Ingredients

Hard-boiled eggs	4, shelled and finely chopped
Cooked white rice	2 Tbsp
Fresh white breadcrumbs	2 Tbsp
Grated Cheddar cheese	2 Tbsp
Chopped fresh parsley	1 Tbsp
Worcestershire sauce	1 tsp
Salt	1 tsp
Ground black pepper	1/2 tsp
Egg	1, white and yolk separated
Dried white breadcrumbs	2 Tbsp
Butter	60 g (2 oz)

Method

- In a large bowl, mix together hard-boiled eggs, rice, fresh breadcrumbs, cheese, parsley, Worcestershire sauce, salt and pepper with a fork.
- Stir in egg yolk and combine well. Shape mixture into small cutlets.
- Beat egg white lightly. Using a pastry brush, lightly coat cutlets with egg white, then roll them in dried breadcrumbs.
- In a pan, melt butter over moderate heat. When foam subsides, place cutlets in pan and fry for 6–8 minutes or until they are golden brown on both sides.
- Remove cutlets from pan, drain on absorbent paper and serve immediately.

N O T E

As a variation to this recipe, 30 g (1 oz) chopped ham may be added to the mixing bowl. You may then reduce the number of hard-boiled eggs used to three.

egg and vegetable flan

This flan is a tasty way to use leftover vegetables. It may be served either hot or cold.

Serves 4

Ingredients

Pastry

Plain (all-purpose) flour	170 g (5½ oz)
Salt	a dash
Butter	45 g (1½ oz), cut into small cubes
Vegetable shortening	45 g (1½ oz), cut into small cubes
Cold water	1–2 Tbsp

Filling

Butter	45 g (1½ oz)
Onion	1 small, peeled and finely chopped
Plain (all-purpose) flour	2 Tbsp
Milk	315 ml (10½ fl oz / 1¼ cups)
Potato	1, large, peeled, cooked and sliced
Carrot	1, large, peeled, cooked and diced
Green peas	2 Tbsp, blanched
Salt	½ tsp
Ground white pepper	¼ tsp
Hard-boiled eggs	4, shelled and sliced
Grated Cheddar cheese	55 g (2 oz)

Method

- Prepare pastry. Sift flour and salt into a mixing bowl. Add butter and vegetable shortening. Rub fat into flour with your fingertips until mixture resembles fine breadcrumbs.

- Add 1 Tbsp cold water and, using a table knife, mix it into flour mixture. Knead dough until smooth. Add more water if dough is too dry. Refrigerate for 30 minutes.

- Preheat oven to 200°C (400°F).

- Roll out pastry to 0.5-cm (¼-in) thickness and ease it into a 20-cm (8-in) flan or pie dish. Trim edges with a knife. Cover pastry with aluminium foil and a layer of dried beans.

- Bake pastry blind for 15 minutes, then remove aluminium foil and dried beans. Set pastry case aside to cool.

- Preheat grill (broiler) to high.

- Prepare filling. In a small saucepan, melt butter over moderate heat. When foam subsides, fry onion for 5–7 minutes or until onion is soft.

- Remove pan from heat. With a wooden spoon, stir in flour to make a smooth paste. Gradually add milk, stirring constantly.

- Return pan to heat and, still stirring, bring sauce to the boil. Simmer for 2–3 minutes or until sauce is thick and smooth. Stir in potato, carrot, peas, salt and pepper.

- Line bottom of pastry case with egg slices. Pour sauce over and sprinkle with cheese. Place flan under grill for 3–4 minutes or until top is lightly browned. Serve hot or cold.

NOTE

This flan can be served hot or cold. Serve immediately after grilling, if you wish to serve it hot. Otherwise, allow flan to cool to room temperature, then refrigerate for 30 minutes before serving.

scrambled eggs with chilli

This is a dish prepared by the Parsi community of western India. Serve it on freshly toasted bread for brunch.

Serves 4

Ingredients

Butter	45 g (1½ oz)
Onion	1, medium-sized, peeled and finely chopped
Ginger	2.5-cm (1-in), peeled and finely chopped
Green chilli	1, finely chopped
Ground turmeric	½ tsp
Chopped coriander leaves (cilantro)	1½ Tbsp
Salt	½ tsp
Eggs	8, lightly beaten
Tomatoes	2, sliced
White bread	4 slices, toasted

Method

- In a medium-sized pan, melt butter over moderate heat. When foam subsides, fry onion and ginger for 5–7 minutes or until onion is soft and translucent but not brown.
- Add chilli, turmeric, coriander leaves and salt. Stir well and cook mixture for 1 minute.
- Pour in beaten eggs, reduce heat to low and cook, stirring constantly, until they are softly scrambled.
- Place a slice of tomato on each slice of toast. Top with scrambled egg mixture and garnish as desired. Serve immediately.
- For alternative presentation, use a pastry cutter to cut desired shapes out of bread before topping with tomato slices and cooked eggs.

curried eggs

This dish is slightly spicy, with the use of curry powder and sliced red chillies.

Serves 4–6

Ingredients

Cooking oil	2 Tbsp
Shallots	3, peeled and finely sliced
Vegetable curry powder	3 Tbsp
Galangal	1-cm (1/2-in) knob, peeled and bruised
Red chillies	2, sliced
Coconut milk	375 ml (12 fl oz / 1 1/2 cups)
Tomatoes	2, cut into wedges
Hard-boiled eggs	6, shelled

Method

- Heat oil in a wok and stir-fry shallots until lightly browned and fragrant.

- Mix curry powder with some water into a thick paste and add to wok. Stir-fry until fragrant then add galangal, chillies, coconut milk and tomatoes. Allow to simmer.

- Add eggs and cook, stirring, until curry thickens slightly. Garnish as desired and serve hot.

N O T E

For a less spicy dish, seed chillies before using. Always handle chillies with a pair of gloves to avoid getting a burning sensation on your skin.

tea eggs

Although they are similar to hard-boiled eggs, Tea Eggs are lightly fragranced with tea, star anise and cinnamon, and feature a lovely marbled pattern.

Serves 4–6

Ingredients

Eggs	6
Black tea infusion	750 ml (24 fl oz / 3 cups)
Salt	1 tsp
Light soy sauce	2 Tbsp
Star anise	3
Cinnamon stick	2, each 5-cm (2-in) long

Method

- Hard-boil eggs, then soak in cold water until cool.

- Tap hard-boiled eggs gently on a work surface or using the back of a spoon to crack shells all over.

- Bring tea infusion to the boil and stir in salt and soy sauce. Add star anise, cinnamon and eggs. Simmer over low heat for 2 hours. Watch that pot does not dry out as it simmers. Add more water as necessary.

- Shell eggs. Eggs should have a lovely marbled pattern. Serve hot.

egg fried rice

This classic dish is an ideal accompaniment to other Chinese meat and vegetable dishes.

Serves 4

Ingredients

Eggs	2
Light soy sauce	2 tsp
Salt	½ tsp
Spring onions (scallions)	2, finely chopped
Cooking oil	2 Tbsp
Day-old cooked long-grain rice	450 g (1 lb)
Green peas	100 g (3½ oz)

Method

- Break eggs into a bowl and add soy sauce, salt and half the spring onions. Beat lightly to mix well.

- Heat oil in a wok. Add egg mixture and stir until egg is lightly scrambled.

- Add rice and stir-fry to break up any lumps. Add peas and remaining spring onions. Stir-fry to mix well and heat rice through. Serve hot.

NOTE

Fried rice is usually prepared using day-old cooked rice because it is drier and will thus keep its shape while absorbing all the flavours of the ingredients. Freshly cooked rice tends to contain more moisture and thus may become mushy when stir-fried.

quail eggs with mushrooms

This dish is simple to do yet very attractive and tasty.
Serves 5

Ingredients

Dried Chinese mushrooms	10, large, soaked to soften
Cooking oil	2 tsp
Salt	1/4 tsp
Ground white pepper	1/4 tsp
Sugar	1/4 tsp
Quail eggs	10
Green peas	10
Vegetable stock	100 ml (3 1/2 fl oz)
Chinese cooking wine (*hua tiao*)	1 tsp, or dry sherry
Light soy sauce	1 tsp
Sesame oil	1/2 tsp
Corn flour (cornstarch)	1 tsp, mixed with 1 Tbsp water

Method

- Squeeze out any excess water from mushrooms and trim off and discard stems.
- Marinate mushrooms with oil, salt, pepper and sugar. Leave for 5 minutes.
- Place mushrooms with the underside facing up on a steaming plate and steam for 10–12 minutes.
- Break a quail egg into each mushroom and top each with a pea. Return to steamer and steam for another 5 minutes or until eggs are cooked.
- Meanwhile combine stock and wine in a small pot and bring to the boil. Season with soy sauce and sesame oil. Lower heat and stir in corn flour mixture to thicken sauce.
- Pour sauce over mushrooms and serve hot.

chawanmushi
(egg custard)

In Japan, chawanmushi is prepared in special chawanmushi cups with lids. If you don't have these cups, porcelain rice bowls or ramekins will do.

Serves 4

Ingredients

Dashi or chicken stock	435 ml (14½ fl oz / 1¾ cups)
Japanese soy sauce	1 tsp
Mirin	1 tsp
Salt	½ tsp
Eggs	3, lightly beaten
Fresh shiitake mushroom	1, cut into 4 slices
Edamame	4, pods removed

Method

- Mix together dashi or chicken stock, soy sauce, mirin, salt and eggs in a bowl.
- Divide egg mixture equally among 4 cups and drop a slice of mushroom into each.
- Cover cups with lids or aluminium foil, then steam for 5 minutes. Do not use too high a heat or eggs will curdle and become tough.
- Reduce heat and leave to steam for another 12–15 minutes or until mixture is set.
- Drop an edamame into each cup as garnish. Serve hot.

snacks & desserts

custard tart

A smooth, creamy, delicately flavoured custard in a rich shortcrust pastry shell.

Serves 4

Ingredients

Plain (all-purpose) flour	170 g (5½ oz)
Salt	a dash
Butter	115 g (4 oz) + 1 tsp
Castor (superfine) sugar	2 tsp
Egg yolk	1, small, lightly beaten
Cold water	1–2 Tbsp

Custard

Egg	1
Egg yolks	2
Sugar	2 Tbsp
Plain (all-purpose) flour	1 Tbsp
Milk	160 ml (5½ fl oz)
Single (light) cream	160 ml (5½ fl oz)
Butter	1 Tbsp, melted
Vanilla essence (extract)	1 tsp

Method

- Preheat oven to 200°C (400°F).

- Sift flour and salt into a mixing bowl. Add 115 g (4 oz) butter and cut it into small pieces with a table knife. Rub flour and butter together with your fingertips until mixture resembles fine breadcrumbs. Mix in sugar.

- Add beaten egg yolk with 1 Tbsp cold water and mix with the knife. With your hands, mix and knead dough until smooth. Add more water if dough is too dry. Chill dough in the refrigerator for 30 minutes.

- Using remaining butter, grease a 17.5–20-cm (7–8-in) flan tin with a removable bottom.

- Roll out pastry 5 cm (2 in) larger in diameter than flan tin, then ease into tin and trim edges. Refrigerate for 10 minutes.

- Remove lined tin from refrigerator and bake blind (see pg 104) for 10 minutes. Remove from oven and set aside to cool.

- Lower oven temperature to 170°C (340°F).

- Prepare custard. In a mixing bowl, beat egg, egg yolks and sugar together until mixture is thick and pale in colour. Mix in flour, then milk, cream, melted butter and vanilla essence.

- Pour into pastry case and bake for 45–50 minutes or until custard is light brown and set. If pastry or filling browns too quickly, cover with a piece of aluminium foil to prevent burning.

- Let tart cool for 10 minutes before removing from tin. Serve cold.

jam omelette

This makes an interesting dessert. Any thick jam may be used but a dark-coloured fruit jam, such as raspberry, will look more attractive than a pale one, such as apricot.

Serves 2

Ingredients

Eggs	4
Castor (superfine) sugar	$\frac{1}{2}$ Tbsp
Salt	a dash
Butter	30 g (1 oz)
Thick jam	2 Tbsp

Method

- In a mixing bowl, beat eggs, sugar and salt together.
- In a pan, melt butter over moderate heat. When foam subsides, pour in egg mixture.
- Tilt and rotate pan to allow liquid mixture to run from the centre to the edges.
- When omelette begins to set, place jam on one half of omelette, leaving edges clear.
- With a spatula or palette knife, fold omelette over and slide it onto a cutting board. Cut omelette in half and serve immediately.

rich chocolate cream

This mouthwatering chocolate cream can be served with any toppping of choice.

Serves 4

Ingredients

Dark (semi-sweet) cooking chocolate — 115 g (4 oz), broken into small pieces

Castor (superfine) sugar — 55 g (2 oz)

Milk — 315 ml (10½ fl oz / 1¼ cups)

Egg yolks — 4

Dark rum or brandy — 3 Tbsp

Double (heavy) cream — 315 ml (10½ fl oz / 1¼ cups)

Topping

Cocoa powder (optional)

Icing (confectioner's) sugar (optional)

Method

- Place chocolate, sugar and milk in a heavy saucepan. Set over low heat and cook, stirring frequently, for 3–5 minutes or until sugar has dissolved and chocolate has melted. Remove from heat and set aside.

- Beat egg yolks in a heatproof (flameproof) mixing bowl. Gradually add milk mixture, beating constantly.

- Set bowl in a pan half-filled with hot water. Set pan over low heat and cook mixture, stirring constantly with a wooden spoon, until mixture coats the back of the spoon. This will take some time.

- Remove pan from heat. Lift bowl out of pan. Stir in rum or brandy and set aside to cool completely, stirring occasionally.

- Pour cream into another mixing bowl and beat until stiff peaks form. Fold cream into cooled chocolate custard, blending thoroughly.

- Pour mixture into a chilled glass serving bowl or individual glasses and refrigerate for 4 hours.

- Sprinkle with topping ingredients or decorate as desired before serving.

chocolate egg custard

This rich and nutritious dish, flavoured with cocoa, is always a favourite with children. Serve as a light snack at any time of the day.

Serves 6–8

Ingredients

Milk	500 ml (16 fl oz / 2 cups)
Large eggs	4
Sugar	4 Tbsp
Cocoa powder	4 Tbsp

Method

- Combine all ingredients in a bowl and whisk until ingredients are well mixed.
- Pour mixture into 6–8 ramekins and cover with aluminium foil.
- Place ramekins in a steamer and steam over rapidly boiling water for 20 minutes or until custard is set.
- Remove from heat. If serving hot, serve immediately. If serving cold, leave to cool to room temperature before refrigerating for 30–45 minutes.

egg puffs with custard

These light puffs are ideal served at parties. Omit the custard and fill them with ice cream for a great treat for children.

Makes 15–20 puffs

Ingredients

Choux Pastry

Water	250 ml (8 fl oz / 1 cup)
Sugar	1 tsp
Butter	125 g (4$^1/_2$ oz)
Plain (all-purpose) flour	140 g (5 oz), sifted
Eggs	4

Custard

Custard powder	60 g (2 oz)
Sugar	80 g (2$^1/_2$ oz)
Milk	500 ml (16 fl oz / 2 cups)
Vanilla essence (extract)	1 tsp

Method

- Bring water to the boil in a pot and add sugar. Stir to melt sugar. Return to the boil and add butter. Stir until completely melted.
- Reduce heat and pour in flour all at once, stirring to incorporate. You should get a smooth batter that leaves the sides of the pot.
- Leave batter to cool slightly before beating in eggs, one at a time. Ensure egg is completely incorporated before adding the next one.
- Pipe or spoon small mounds of batter onto a baking tray.
- Bake in a preheated oven at 220°C (440°F) for 15 minutes, then reduce heat to 150°C (300°F) and bake for another 10 minutes.
- Remove puffs from tray immediately to avoid sticking.
- Combine custard ingredients in a pan and stir until well mixed. Cook over medium heat, stirring until custard thickens. Refrigerate until chilled before using.
- When puffs are slightly cooled, make a slit in each one and fill with custard. Serve immediately.

fu chok
tong shui

This is a Chinese dessert that can be served both hot or cold. Adjust the amount of sugar used to your personal preference.

Serves 4

Ingredients

Bean curd sticks	180 g (6 oz), soaked to soften and drained
Canned ginkgo nuts	30
Rock sugar	125 g (4½ oz)
Water	1 litre (32 fl oz / 4 cups)
Eggs	2, lightly beaten

Method

- Break or cut bean curd sticks into shorter lengths and place in a pot.

- Add all other ingredients, except eggs.

- Bring to the boil and simmer for about 1 hour 30 minutes or until bean curd sticks are very soft and broken up.

- Turn off heat and pour egg into soup in a slow steady stream about 10–12.5 cm (4–5 in) above pot while stirring in a single direction to form thin ribbons.

- If serving hot, ladle into individual bowls and serve immediately. If serving cold, leave to cool slightly before refrigerating for about 1 hour.

Using canned ginkgo nuts is convenient as it does away with the need to shell the fresh nuts, and to soak them and remove their skins and bitter shoots.

spanish caramel custard

This traditional Spanish dessert is essentially a custard lightly flavoured with orange and coated with caramel.

Serves 4

Ingredients

Milk	625 ml (20 fl oz / 2½ cups)
Sugar	175 g (6 oz)
Eggs	4
Orange zest	2 tsp
Water	2 Tbsp
Hot water	

Method

- Heat milk and 50 g (2 oz) sugar together until sugar dissolves. Leave to cool.

- Beat eggs well and add orange zest. Pour sweetened milk into eggs, whisking thoroughly. Set aside.

- Preheat oven to 180°C (350°F).

- To make caramel, heat remaining sugar in a clean, dry saucepan until it dissolves and turns a rich golden brown. Do not stir but swirl around the pan if necessary. When caramel reaches the right shade, remove from heat and stir in 2 Tbsp water. The caramel will bubble up, so be careful.

- Working quickly, hold moulds with an oven glove and pour a little caramel into each ramekin, swirling it around to coat the sides.

- Strain custard to remove orange zest and carefully pour into ramekins. Stand them in a baking dish and pour in enough hot water to rise halfway up the sides of ramekins. Place in the oven for 30 minutes.

- To test if custard is done, insert a skewer into the centre. The skewer should come out clean. Remove from hot water and allow to cool before refrigerating.

- To serve custard, cover each ramekin with a small upturned plate. Carefully turn over and lift off ramekin.

coconut macaroons

These classic cakes are moist and chewy. Serve with a hot cup of tea.
Makes 18

Ingredients

Desiccated coconut	225 g (7½ oz)
Castor (superfine) sugar	275 g (9 oz)
Egg whites	5
Butter for greasing	
Glacé (candied) cherries	9, halved

Method

- Preheat oven to 180°C (350°F).
- Mix coconut, sugar and egg whites together in a small saucepan and place over low heat until mixture is warm but not hot. Stir constantly with a wooden spoon.
- Remove pan from heat and leave mixture to cool in pan.
- Grease a baking tray and cover with greaseproof paper.
- Using a tablespoon, spoon 18 mounds of mixture onto greaseproof paper, leaving enough space in between for macaroons to expand during baking. Alternatively, spoon into baking cups.
- Top each macaroon with half a glacé cherry, then bake for 20 minutes or until light golden brown. Remove from oven and leave baking tray to cool on a wire rack.
- If using greaseproof paper, peel it off baking tray and cut between cooled macaroons. Leave a layer of paper on the base of each macaroon. Store in an airtight container.

Instead of shaping the macaroons into mounds, you can also press them down slightly to flatten them. This will make the macaroons slightly crispier.

baked chinese cake

These small cakes are somewhat like the sponge cake, but drier as cooking oil is used in place of butter.

Makes 8

Ingredients

Large eggs	3
Castor (superfine) sugar	140 g (5 oz)
Honey	1 Tbsp
Ovalette	1 tsp
Water	3 Tbsp
Vanilla essence (extract)	1 tsp
Cooking oil	70 ml (2$\frac{1}{2}$ fl oz)
Plain (all-purpose) flour	160 g (5$\frac{1}{2}$ oz), sifted
Corn flour (cornstarch)	1 Tbsp, sifted
Baking powder	1 tsp, sifted

Method

- Preheat oven to 180°C (350°F). Grease 8 baking cups, each 10 x 5 cm (4 x 2 in), then lightly coat with flour.
- Beat eggs, sugar, honey and ovalette together until mixture is light and fluffy.
- Add water, vanilla essence and oil. Mix well.
- Fold in both flours and baking powder, then spoon batter into prepared baking cups.
- Bake for 15 minutes. Turn baking cups over to pop cakes out of cups. Leave to cool slightly before serving.

As with other cake and cup cake recipes, you can also use moulds of different shapes and sizes to bake this Chinese cake.

glossary

1. Bean curd sticks

Made from boiling soy milk, then lifting the skin that forms on the surface and drying it. These brittle, cream-coloured sticks are commonly used in braised dishes, soups and desserts. Like bean curd, it is a gluten-free food.

2. Black moss

This coarse black vegetable is also known as hair moss or hair vegetable. It is actually a freshwater algae and is popularly used in Chinese cooking, especially during the Chinese new year. This is because its Chinese name, *fa cai*, means "wealth", a good omen for the festive occasion. Black moss is relatively bland and takes on the flavour of the ingredients it is cooked with readily.

3. Black sesame seeds

These small, flat, tear-drop shaped seeds have a nutty flavour and are used in both sweet and savoury dishes. Sesame seeds have a high oil content and can be stored in an airtight container in a cool, dark place for up to 3 months. Substitute with white sesame seeds if unavailable, although the black variety is more flavourful. White sesame seeds are often toasted before use to enhance their flavour.

4. Candlenuts

These hard nuts have a high oil content and were once used to make candles. They are usually crushed or ground and used as a thickening agent in curries or sauces. Store in the refrigerator.

5. Century eggs

Century eggs are made from duck eggs. Fresh duck eggs are covered in a paste of leaves, ash, lime, salt and water and then left to cure for a few weeks. Scrape off the paste and wash the eggs before using. The shelled egg will reveal a dark, translucent white and a creamy, dark green yolk with a rather pungent flavour. Century eggs do not require cooking.

6. Chinese cooking wine

Made from fermented glutinous rice, Chinese cooking wine was originally from Shao Xing in Zhejiang province, and so the wine is today also commonly known as Shao Xing wine. Store in a cool, dark place, away from direct sunlight.

7. Coconut milk

This is not to be confused with the watery coconut juice found in the inside of a fresh coconut. Coconut milk is obtained from squeezing grated coconut flesh with warm water. The white milk is fragrant and is used to flavour many sweet and savoury Asian dishes. Coconut milk or coconut cream, a thicker version, are available pre-packed from supermarkets. Thin down coconut cream with water until the consistency of milk is achieved.

8. Courgettes (zucchini)

Courgettes look somewhat like long slender cucumbers and the skin colour can vary from dark to light green. A yellow variety is also available. The flesh is a light, cream colour and the flavour is delicate. Courgettes can be eaten raw, baked, grilled or sautéed.

9. Dried Chinese mushrooms

These are dried shiitake mushrooms. They have a more robust, earthy flavour compared to fresh shiitake mushrooms, but must be soaked in warm water for at least 30 minutes to soften before use. The stems are usually trimmed and discarded as they are too tough to be eaten.

10. Dried instant yeast

Available as tiny granules sealed in foil envelopes, dried instant yeast is dormant but can be activated with warm water or moisture. Store in a cool, dark place or in the refrigerator.

11. Edamame

These are fresh soy beans, often sold still in their bright green pods. The pods are short and often contain only two to three beans. Edamame is often served simply steamed and salted then removed from the pods and eaten.

12. Fresh Shiitake mushrooms

These fresh mushrooms are large and meaty and are often used as a meat substitute in vegetarian dishes. They are commonly stir-fried or used in soups but are milder in flavour than the dried variety.

13. Ground turmeric

This is the powdered version of fresh turmeric. Easily identified by its brilliant yellow-orange colour, ground turmeric has a pungent but pleasant flavour and is commonly used in curries. As with all ground spices, store in a cool, dark place. Turmeric stains easily, so handle with care.

14. Lemon grass

Also known as citronella, lemon grass has a fresh, lemony flavour. It is usually added to curries or stews for the length of cooking time and then removed before the dish is served, since it cannot be eaten. Cut off and discard the green upper stalks and use only the lower bulbous stem. Crush or bruise to get the most of its flavour.

15. Nutmeg

This hard, light brown oblong-shaped seed is about 2.5-cm (1-in) long. Its flavour is warm and sweet. Although nutmeg is available ground, freshly grated nutmeg is superior and should be used where possible. Grate nutmeg with a small kitchen grater.

16. Ovalette

Ovalette is a cake emulsifier and it is added to cake batters to give cakes a lighter, more voluminous texture. It is available at some supermarkets and most baking specialty stores.

17. Salted eggs

Salted eggs are made from duck eggs. The fresh eggs are coated with a paste made from clay, salt and water and then left for a few weeks. Salted eggs are usually sold, still coated with the paste. Scrape off the paste and wash the eggs before using. Raw salted eggs have a clear runny white and hard, yellow yolk. Salted eggs are usually hard-boiled. The yolks are also used to add a salty flavour to Chinese pastries.

18. Turmeric

As with the ground version, this root spice has a pungent but pleasant flavour, and an incredible staining ability. Handle with care. Its thin, light brown skin often allows its bright orange flesh to peek through, so it is easily identifiable. Scrape off the thin brown skin before using.

19. Vegetable shortening

This is a solid fat made from vegetable oils and is white in colour. Vegetable shortening is flavourless and unlike butter, it can be stored at room temperature. It is used as with butter, in baking or cooking.

20. White button mushrooms

These mushrooms are round and have short, thick stems. They can be eaten raw but are also often cooked as this helps enhance their flavour. Most cooks simply wipe it clean before use, although some prefer to peel off the top layer from the caps.

Weights and Measures

Quantities for this book are given in Metric, Imperial and American (spoon and cup) measures. Standard spoon and cup measurements used are: 1 tsp = 5 ml, 1 Tbsp = 15 ml, 1 cup = 250 ml. All measures are level unless otherwise stated.

Liquid And Volume Measures

Metric	Imperial	American
5 ml	$1/6$ fl oz	1 teaspoon
10 ml	$1/3$ fl oz	1 dessertspoon
15 ml	$1/2$ fl oz	1 tablespoon
60 ml	2 fl oz	$1/4$ cup (4 tablespoons)
85 ml	$2^1/_2$ fl oz	$1/3$ cup
90 ml	3 fl oz	$3/8$ cup (6 tablespoons)
125 ml	4 fl oz	$1/2$ cup
180 ml	6 fl oz	$3/4$ cup
250 ml	8 fl oz	1 cup
300 ml	10 fl oz ($1/2$ pint)	$1^1/_4$ cups
375 ml	12 fl oz	$1^1/_2$ cups
435 ml	14 fl oz	$1^3/_4$ cups
500 ml	16 fl oz	2 cups
625 ml	20 fl oz (1 pint)	$2^1/_2$ cups
750 ml	24 fl oz ($1^1/_5$ pints)	3 cups
1 litre	32 fl oz ($1^3/_5$ pints)	4 cups
1.25 litres	40 fl oz (2 pints)	5 cups
1.5 litres	48 fl oz ($2^2/_5$ pints)	6 cups
2.5 litres	80 fl oz (4 pints)	10 cups

Dry Measures

Metric	Imperial
30 grams	1 ounce
45 grams	$1^1/_2$ ounces
55 grams	2 ounces
70 grams	$2^1/_2$ ounces
85 grams	3 ounces
100 grams	$3^1/_2$ ounces
110 grams	4 ounces
125 grams	$4^1/_2$ ounces
140 grams	5 ounces
280 grams	10 ounces
450 grams	16 ounces (1 pound)
500 grams	1 pound, $1^1/_2$ ounces
700 grams	$1^1/_2$ pounds
800 grams	$1^3/_4$ pounds
1 kilogram	2 pounds, 3 ounces
1.5 kilograms	3 pounds, $4^1/_2$ ounces
2 kilograms	4 pounds, 6 ounces

Length

Metric	Imperial
0.5 cm	$1/4$ inch
1 cm	$1/2$ inch
1.5 cm	$3/4$ inch
2.5 cm	1 inch

Oven Temperature

	°C	°F	Gas Regulo
Very slow	120	250	1
Slow	150	300	2
Moderately slow	160	325	3
Moderate	180	350	4
Moderately hot	190/200	375/400	5/6
Hot	210/220	410/425	6/7
Very hot	230	450	8
Super hot	250/290	475/550	9/10

Abbreviation

tsp	teaspoon
Tbsp	tablespoon
g	gram
kg	kilogram
ml	millilitre